Don't Be Brave

Uncensored Motivational Quotes

S. SULIANAH

Praise for Be Brave: Uncensored Motivational Quotes

Sulianah *(Be Brave: Uncensored Motivational Quotes)* offers a compendium of original maxims, thoughts, and advice for readers eager for continual inspiration, with the promise that, even when the material gets frank or challenging, the author will resist the urge to censor. Sharing a few lines or even short paragraphs on each page on a host of topics, Sulianah urges readers toward self love and acceptance *("Believe in yourself even though others do not believe in you")*, overcoming self doubt *("You can overcome anything in your life. The question is whether you want to")*, and understanding and even exiting unhealthy relationships *("Do not make compromises when others devalue you as a person.")*

The result reads like the advice a friend might want to offer to someone caught in an unhealthy relationship or situation but at times, out of politeness, might soft-pedal. No soft-pedaling here, though: *"If someone cannot accept who you are, why are you desperate to be who they want you to be?"* asks Sulianah, whose experience as a poet shines through in the crisp, direct, at times epigrammatic prose. While generally upbeat and encouraging, Sulianah's straight talk at times comes with sharp elbows: one chapter is titled *"Confidently Respond to Certified Idiots,"* which addresses situations like the boss who won't listen, acquaintances who ask to borrow money, and how to respond when someone raises their voice.

— *Publishers Weekly Reviewer*
BookLife Reviews

ALSO BY S.SULIANAH

Poetry
Letters of a Thousand Speeches
Masterpiece in Your Heart

WHEN YOU NEED TO *Be Brave*

⟶ Love Yourself   *13*

⟶ Be Yourself   *27*

⟶ Persistently Pursue Your Dreams   *41*

⟶ Make Decisions   *69*

⟶ Overcome Your Self-Doubts   *75*

⟶ Acknowledge Your Instincts   *85*

⟶ Be Charming   *95*

⟶ Leave a Relationship   *117*

⟶ Move on from Someone You Are in Love With   *139*

⟶ Confidently Respond to Certified Idiots   *151*

Hello My Dear Readers:

The idea to create this book came to me while writing my first personality development book, *Breaking Your Own Boundaries*.

Growing up, I learnt many new things by reading, and my curiosity has given me opportunities throughout the years to test and observe whether what I have read can be practically applied to my life.

I find myself energized by the things I look forward to every day — even as simple as waking up and having breakfast. Every time I feel like giving up on my goals, quotes and advice from motivational speakers and people who have already reached such stages in their lives encourage me to continue striving.

I have always appreciated writers' experiences and their commitment to sharing them in writing. Therefore, I decided to write these quotes based on my personal

Be Brave

experiences, without censoring any words, to motivate you in some way.

Most of the time, I make sure that anything I say does not hurt the feelings of others. I am also known as someone who is careful and selective in what I share with others, including my opinions.

My friends often ask me, *'How can you be so calm and patient in stressful situations?'* This usually happens while giving presentations, during exams or when dealing with difficult people. When I am nervous, I think about what I plan to do after the event, like going to a cafe or watching a movie, so I can focus on something other than what makes me anxious. Thinking about how this book can motivate readers, I am able to break through my wall of nervousness and hesitation and gather the courage to express my uncensored thoughts.

When you read *Be Brave: Uncensored Motivational Quotes*, I hope you find the assurance to be self-aware of your strengths and holistic disposition, to be brave in your decision-making and to accept and appreciate yourself. I hope you will be brave when defending your rights and yourself, and I hope these words will somehow motivate you when you feel down in the same way they helped me.

WHEN YOU NEED TO
BE BRAVE
TO LOVE YOURSELF

Learning to understand how you behave in situations, recognizing how your feelings develop and being self-aware of the way your mind operates are the first steps to appreciating yourself.

It takes faith and determination to understand your personality and to build on it throughout your life. You need courage and strong self-perception to accept yourself when others don't.

Your self-worth is in the highest tier of your priorities. Not even your parents or your partner are allowed to make you feel down about yourself.

Focus on building your self-esteem and the way you perceive yourself. This is a vital step to attaining happiness and peace of mind.

Throughout the journey of attaining your purpose in life, be observant.

Open your mind and emotions to learn how your body works and harness this knowledge.

Observe how you make decisions in life. Analyse the patterns of how your mind and feelings work in situations.

When you feel dejected, be self-aware of these feelings. Ask yourself why you have these emotions and how you can manage them to avoid them affecting you in the long-term.

The first step to healing is acknowledging your feelings.

You might have noticed a pattern in your behaviour. Observe and draw a mind map. Then, analyse whether this is what you want to be as a person. If not, change.

Try this method, especially when you identify that certain behaviours tend to not make you feel good, such as when you keep changing your mind at the last minute or avoid responsibilities.

Drawing a mind map is a way to rewind memories of past decisions you made and to observe behaviours and outcomes that are consistent.

When you draw these experiences in a mind map, you will notice repetitions. Once you see the root cause or bottleneck that made you fickle-minded, you can use it the next time you are attempting to improve yourself.

The last time I used this method was when I felt strong romantic feelings for other people. Instead of telling them about my feelings, I kept avoiding them and I was not sure if they felt the same way as I did. How would I know that they never felt the same? Did I ever ask them?

No. Never.

Each time, I either continued to be friends with them and let the feelings fade or fell out of touch. After drawing my most recent mind map, I decided to change. Instead of keeping it to myself, I told the recent two I had feelings for them. I realized one reason for my behaviour is that I continue falling for people who are unavailable, because I am not ready to be in a committed relationship, whether the person is taken or not.

Hence, I continued to have excuses. Before it became real, I usually let it go. So, I found the root cause of my behaviour through a written mind map.

You can do this too. Change the way you think and the way you do things if you are beginning to notice too much repetition in your life.

Do not rely on your partner completely for everything. One day, in the event you are no longer together, you will need to have the courage to continue your life outside the relationship.

Believe in yourself even though others do not believe in you. Your perception of yourself is the only thing that matters.

Have you ever noticed times when you find it difficult to make a decision or you change your opinions based on the external environment and influences? Well, this usually means that your mind and feelings are not working together.

Your mind might be reminding you of the principles you have, while your feelings are telling you to do something you like.

You don't owe anyone anything.

Therefore, you can choose what to say and who to tell about what is going on in your life.

Making yourself and your safety a priority are not the acts of a selfish person. You need to make choices for your well-being instead of worrying about how your decisions may hurt the feelings of others or impact your relationship with them. This is usually a moment when deep inside, you know that enough is enough and that it is now time to focus on your happiness.

WHEN YOU NEED TO
BE BRAVE
TO BE YOURSELF

At one point in your life, you will not care about what others think or want you to be. Not everyone will have the opportunity to experience this – only those with the courage to not care about others' opinions.

They said *you should be like her*. They said *she looks better than you*. They asked you *why you can't be like her*. It is hurtful to listen to these remarks, especially when they come from people you spend a lot of time with.

How you wish you could tell them to be more careful when expressing their feelings! Right? Then, tell them. Let them know you don't like being treated or talked to in that way, and if they are sincere about your relationship, they will change. If they insist on not changing, you know the answer: you deserve someone better.

Do not do things that someone else wants you to do to conform to society's conditions.

The first answers for any actions that you need to accomplish are within you.

Why do you feel inferior, especially when talking with other people, like your friends or colleagues?

Is it because you feel as if they are better than you? Is it because you feel like you are a nobody in comparison to them? Is it because you feel like your talent is nothing compared to theirs?

If you are feeling this way, you must learn to eradicate these thoughts and feelings. Change the way you speak to yourself and stop comparing yourself to others.

Be self-dependent.

This will help your self-esteem and confidence flourish to be ready for the unexpected.

Your principles can be your stance on not breaking up relationships just because you are interested in someone.

Principles can be your preferences, such as not preferring to wear an outfit that does not define your identity.

Do not compromise your own choices to fit the trends or others' expectations.

If someone cannot accept who you are, why are you desperate to be who they want you to be?

Do you think they would change to who you want them to be? No, they will not.

So, why are you trying so hard to be accepted by them?

Why are you worried about what others think about you?

No one cares about that new car you just bought. No one cares whether you are travelling around the world. They might see or comment on your social media post or even wish you *all the best* when they meet you in person, but if you don't show the posts, do you think they think about you every minute and wonder what you are doing? Not at all.

So, why are you even worrying about what they think of you?

There is no need to announce to the whole world the things you are doing or have achieved. Learn to be selective about what you share and who you share your accomplishments with.

Why are you worried that your friends or others will talk behind your back? Let it be. Let them talk. You don't need to know the reason they talk behind your back, and it is better for you not to know.

When you reach a crossroad of whether to listen to someone who wants you to be someone you are not and being yourself, ask this question of yourself: *If I were to ever lose something in my life, would that person be there to support me?* If not, you don't need to be who they want you to be.

WHEN YOU NEED TO BE BRAVE TO PERSISTENTLY PURSUE YOUR DREAMS

Be patient.

Be patient when exploring something new in your life. It takes time to adapt to the changes in the environment and your routine, but the results will change your life.

Be patient when dealing with people.

Their behaviour towards you can test your patience. And, yes, patience has its limits.

Think intelligently.

Evaluate wisely.

Be confident.

Be brave.

Be patient when venturing into building your business, clientele and sales.

Observe and test not only the markets but also the services you are providing, your whole entity and your interests.

Change your tactics when needed. Be open to trying new strategies. Your imaginings can become reality if given a chance. You can be patient with people who pissed you off, so why not be patient with yourself and give yourself a chance?

Are you afraid of failing if you do something different than the usual? Well, that is common. All of us feel this way. But remember that the probability of failing and being successful are the same.

Try. Do it anyway. How will you know you will fail without trying?

If you don't set out to accomplish something now, then when?

Overcome your procrastination immediately without allowing other thoughts to dominate you.

You may have internal worries, such as '*What if I fail?*' or '*Why do it anyway if I am not going to make it?*'.

Take that one first step, and it will change the way you think.

There is no need for you to tell everyone your plans, especially when deep inside, you know that their comments and unnecessary personal opinions will cause negativity. Act quietly and strive towards your dreams.

The imagination is a strong, expansive magnetic pull of energy. In seconds, what you are thinking right now could happen. What does imagination become without action? Just a fantasy?

You notice a gorgeous woman a few feet away from you talking to one of your friends, and you think, *'Wow, she is the most beautiful person I have ever seen. I would like to at least say hello to her'*. Imagine this now. In seconds, she ends her conversation with your friend and approaches you. Don't be surprised when she smiles and says hello to you. This is what imagination can do in a matter of seconds as long as your mind and feelings are in tune with each other.

Live the life you have imagined for yourself and be grateful once you accomplish what you wanted.

Anything you have decided to do in this life is your choice. You have control over it. Whatever you are doing now is what you have imagined your life to be, or it can be a journey that you need to take to the point you have in mind.

Be brave when sowing the seeds of your imagination. You will not lose anything by being highly ambitious.

Having a goal is the first step to waking up every morning.

Be curious enough to find your purpose in life.

Having a goal that you see yourself heading towards will make it easier for you to handle all the difficult people you will meet in your life.

Be brave when aiming high, even for a goal twenty years in the future. Define the intent and focus and put in the effort and work towards it.

Relax your mind. Stop when you need a break. Get your ass up. Enjoy the moments but stay focused.

Believe that you will achieve the goal, provided both your thoughts and feelings agree with the decision.

Show up. Arrive at work on time. Finish the tasks you are planning to do.

Be disciplined. This is evidence that you are making efforts to treasure yourself.

Sometimes, situations prevent you from running your business or working on other interests full-time. Resolve it by doing it part-time. When the time comes, you can commit fully to the goal. Put your mind and heart into your intention, and eventually, you will attain it.

Set goals before preparing for any exam.

Compose your mind and heart to imagine the moments when you are preparing for your exam. Learn to understand the concepts, memorize formulas and apply the methods with possible scenarios.

Play the following imagination scenario the day before:

You enter the hall, get your supplies ready at your table, look around to see your friends doing the same, let yourself hear your own breathing, feel the calmness in your mind and heartbeat and let go of the *what-ifs* to eliminate your anxiety.

You are now holding the exam paper, feeling the paper between your fingers, flipping it open and browsing through the exam questions that are familiar, exactly like the ones you prepared. You feel confident that you are answering all the questions with certainty and accuracy, smiling and checking again after you have finished every section for possible mistakes. You complete everything right before the exam ends.

After submitting your paper, you and your friends happily chat outside the hall before going for lunch together to celebrate.

Now, imagine yourself receiving the results. You get the marks you aimed for, contented and satisfied that all your efforts and visions were fruitful.

Be brave when putting your plans and imaginings into action even if you know that it will be tough and you will have to go through obstacles and criticisms.

Set your goals, and you do you!

Whenever you feel like giving up, stop whatever you are doing and free your mind.

Meditate. Pray. Read.

Sleep. Breathe. Exercise. Walk.

Come back to the things you are doing only after your mind is well-rested.

Every time you find that it is becoming challenging to live your life, stop whatever you are doing. Breathe in and out. Look around and admire how the trees grow, how humans walk and talk, how the sun shines at an angle of hope.

Get a book you like and spend your time reading it.

Write what you are feeling at that moment. Write what kind of life you want to live.

Listen to the music of nature while reading and writing.

Cook for yourself.

Gradually, you will get back on your feet.

Thinking too much and worrying too much are two different approaches.

It is okay to think about a situation before it happens just so you can be prepared, but worrying too much will make you less confident about yourself, and more importantly, will prevent you from embracing the moment.

At times, you might encounter obstacles, like when you thought your parents or your partner were a barrier to achieving your goals of travelling solo, doing what you truly love or running your own business. You begin to think the plans are not achievable. Those are B.S. excuses you created for yourself, and you will likely not do what you want to do anyway whether they agree or not.

Learn to find ways that will make them come to terms with your decisions, like letting them imagine the regrets over the years if you don't do it now.

Everyone we meet in our life, whether by chance or not, are usually introduced to us for a reason. You may need them, or they may need you to help in some part of life.

Maybe you are worried about leaving the company you worked at for the past ten years, but that morning your cab driver tells you about his experiences when he was younger. He left his company after working there for decades because his ex-boss did not appreciate his effort. When he realized it was not worth staying, he left and found a place with better benefits and a boss who appreciated him in every way possible.

There was an unbelievable moment I experienced during my bachelor's degree program in psychology. I had an unpleasant time in the beginning of my studies because my grades for every psychology thesis I wrote were either *B*'s or *C*'s. I found it stressful because I used to have good grades when I was writing reports for my business management diploma.

I assumed that the change in my school environment,

working full-time while studying, the gap year and the style of writing required were the reasons for the grades.

Then, one afternoon, I was having a late lunch at Long John Silver's by myself when an old woman, maybe in her eighties, approached me and asked permission to share my table, even though there were many empty seats in the restaurant. I replied, '*Yeah, sure*', even though my brain was thinking about the possibilities that this old woman could be a con-artist trying to rob me in some way or a ghost disguised as an old woman.

She started a conversation with me while sipping her medium iced Coke. I didn't ask her anything, but she went straight to telling me about her daughter who had been living alone in Australia for a few years. I asked her what she was doing there. She said, '*She is studying there, taking her degree in psychology*'. Yes, you read that right.

I told her I was studying that now, and she said, '*Yeah, I can guess that*'.

'*You can guess that?*' I questioned.

She replied, with light in her eyes, '*Yes, you show it in your eyes*'.

So, I took the opportunity to ask how her daughter was doing alone. She said her daughter was doing good, and everything was going well better than before. I did not even ask whether her daughter had good grades or how school was going for her. We did not talk about anything else after that before she left, but in that split second, that conversation changed everything. My stance on how I should approach my studies and my motivation to do well shot straight back up.

When you are worried about something that is not going well in your life, like struggling with changes in your workplace, trying to write a better thesis for good grades or finding yourself on the verge of giving up, you might be surprised how a meeting with a random stranger can share exactly the same experience and how they, or in this case her daughter managed to adapt to a new environment. Then, in a split second, your worries will turn into a catalyst to move on, encouraging you to not give up and to keep moving forward.

Open your mind and heart. Be courageous!

While you are on the journey to achieving your dreams and purpose in life, remember to embrace the memories and spend time with people who care for you. Don't worry about making mistakes; rather, learn from them.

WHEN YOU NEED TO
BE BRAVE
TO MAKE DECISIONS

Fickle mindedness can happen when you have no idea what is going on, when you are unsure about the subject or when you do not have any experience with the kind of situation to make a final decision. You could be worried that your decision could affect the entire team or bring everyone down. Well, those worries are valid.

Find time to ponder the situation before making a decision instead of implementing an action prematurely and having to reverse its consequences.

Being fickle shows your lack of credibility. Ask for help when you need it.

Is there any process that you can follow to lead your life? No, right? Well, then why do you need to worry? There are no processes to follow. Even if there is a process, you will ignore anyway.

Lead your own life. Create new paths.

Be brave in making decisions and acting on them. If you don't make it, so what? Is this life a competition?

Being brave is not something that everyone is capable of. Being brave is only meant for someone who does not care about what others think of them.

WHEN YOU NEED TO
BE BRAVE
TO OVERCOME YOUR
SELF-DOUBTS

✓

Every time you doubt yourself, ask this question: *Is it really because I cannot do this or am I worried what others will think of me?*

Most of the time, the reason for being afraid of doing something is because you are too obsessed with what others will think if you fail.

You have the answers to your self-doubts. They are usually right in front of you. You don't see them because you chose not to. You chose to compromise with thoughts like, *'It's okay, not a big deal, don't be too sensitive'*. Then, you let it burn inside you for years.

You can overcome anything in your life. The question is whether you want to.

The first step to understanding why you doubt yourself is acknowledging why something makes you feel that way. Then, you have to make an effort to work on it so you can alleviate the self-doubt, which will eventually make you feel better. Sync your mind and feelings with the issue you have at hand, and it will make a difference in the outcome.

Earlier, I mentioned my struggles with my psychology thesis and that after meeting the mysterious old lady, everything changed.

I had a more positive perspective about what I wanted, and I told myself that I will graduate with good grades, but this changed the perspective of the problem into how I was going to get better when I didn't know how to or the actual reasons. In my opinion, I thought my thesis was well-written in my own style of writing, but apparently, the expectations for a quality psychology thesis are different from a business thesis.

There was this classmate of mine who is now one of

my closest friends. She has exceptional speaking and writing skills. By being exposed to her every day, I find myself wanting to speak well like her. She is so fluent in her conversation that she can be witty and always makes me laugh, which is a difficult task. Apart from that, she is a good writer. Her background studies were in law, and she probably speaks English with her family, which are both good explanations for why she is skilled in the language. At the time, I used her as a model for my goals.

I said to myself and in my daily prayers that I wanted to speak and write as fluently as her. Whatever your beliefs are and however you chose to pray, ensure you provide enough detail. In this case, I specifically mentioned her name and the skills that I saw in her that I would like to improve in myself.

A few days later, I accidentally saw one of her psychology reports. I have no idea why the thesis reports were right in front of me and my classmate. As my classmate snuck a peek to see who got the highest grades in the class, I glanced at my friend's thesis to see how she formed her sentences. It was only a reflex, a quick glance at the paper, and I did not even read a whole paragraph, but from that quick glance, I learned comparatively if I was to write a sentence like, '*The weather is hot*' she wrote hers as something better, like '*The weather is scorching hot*'.

The next step I took was to try writing more like her. Guess what? Like I told you earlier, my psychology thesis grades were usually B's and C's, but after that, they turned into A+'s and A-'s. I used that same formula for my marketing thesis, and I was impressed by how it turned out. An even bigger impact came later as my confidence in writing continued to build. I didn't stop writing. This was a big change in how I started to express my feelings through words, but it was not only about writing but also about the confidence to write and to let friends and strangers read my words. That confidence has encouraged me to write articles related to handwriting analysis, motivation and poems and to even have the courage to publish my writing on my websites and in books.

There is no perfection in anything you do. For sure, there will be mistakes and errors. There is no perfection when you first start anything. The most important thing is to work on your aims, have a goal model, keep practicing and improve whenever you need to.

Get rid of all those excuses that you created for yourself, like *'I don't like my voice'* or *'I will be sharing my deepest secrets and what if my friends and family listen'* or *'My room is not suitable for podcast recording because of the echo'* or *'When I am rich, then I will travel the world'* or *'I am too old'* or *'I am too young'*.

Fight off those excuses and worries. Condition your mind and heart to work together to eliminate your self-doubts.

Possible reasons for doubting yourself can develop at a young age or at any time in your life. So, if you are a parent, an educator, a sibling, a friend or a person who generally has relationships with people, be fully mindful that your words and behaviours along with your sarcasm, laughter and mockery could influence how a person thinks and behaves throughout life.

WHEN YOU NEED TO
BE BRAVE
TO ACKNOWLEDGE
YOUR INSTINCTS

That first impulse you feel about a person is the instant analysis programmed from the interactions between your feelings, thoughts, past experiences, the people you have met, the stories you have heard from people and the stories you have watched and listened to.

Your instincts are based on the data you have been collecting in your subconscious since you've existed in this world.

Trust your instincts.

Be self-aware of your first instinct. This is especially helpful if you sense something is not right about a person or if the energy you feel is uneasy and tense.

When you feel this, avoid trying to justify what your inner voice is telling you from what you see and hear. *'She is attractive'*, *'She seems nice'* or *'It is alright, it is only a small matter'* are the phrases you use when trying to ignore your first instinct.

When you tell yourself, '*Yeah, she will not do it again*', that is a denial, and your inner voice is trying to justify the situation. You are trying so hard to find the good things about a person that you have put aside their actions that hurt you in the first place. Believe it or not, she will do it again.

Develop your skills to observe and analyse human behaviour. When you are walking in the park, observe how people talk to their partners or how they react when seeing someone fall off a bicycle.

When you are in your office, observe your colleagues' postures as they speak to your boss and then observe how they are different when chatting with their team members. Analyse patterns in your colleagues' behaviour, such as the times they arrive and leave, when they make coffee, and their tone of voice.

You never know when you will need this information.

When you are in a meeting, avoid the usual process of writing down what is said because you can get that later from the agenda or the presenter's notes.

Do something different.

Observe the people in the room, and write down what you see: their reactions, how they speak, how they behave when someone says something, their tone of voice, their body language and any other peculiarities.

This data that you are gathering is key knowledge for determining whether your meeting agenda will be implemented successfully. It is also a great way to learn about your co-workers' characters.

M

Be sensitive to your surroundings and the people you encounter in your life. Your senses will alert you to what is going to happen and whether the people you are dealing with can be trusted.

Have you ever experienced a situation which you could not believe was guided by your intuition? For instance, it says to you, *'Please do not tell her about that t-shirt your other friend gave you that is too small. You can tell your other friend later without telling her'*.

Then another part of you says, *'But you all have hung out with one another for ten years, it is time for you to open up and start trusting her'*.

Your first intuition, the one element that has been observing patterns of behaviour surrounding you, is your subconscious that taps into people's hidden emotions and thoughts, the ones your eyes might not be able to detect and that you always try to justify. It is this first intuition that you often decide to push aside. A few weeks later, similar situations occur and you continue justifying them. Only when you realize that something is just too much, do you decide to do something, but it is often too late.

WHEN YOU NEED TO
BE BRAVE
TO BE CHARMING

If no one asks for your opinion, learn to control yourself.

Do not voice your valuable point of view, which they will ignore anyway. Don't waste your time advising others who do not want to hear it.

When someone is talking, learn to control your behaviour and reactions.

Do not interrupt by interjecting with stories about your own life. Give them their moment.

Ignoring someone else's worries and what they are telling you is called gaslighting.

When someone tells you about a problem, listen to them and acknowledge the problem. If you hate to listen to people, learn to do it better. This is a tip to be charming, yes, but also for being a respectable human.

Do not judge and look down on someone who wears simple attire and does not prioritize fancy brands in their closet. You may have no idea about who they are, their life story, their dreams or their success stories. Let them live their life.

Do not judge people who own fancy brands of clothes and accessories. You may have no idea what is in their mind. Owning those brands could be their dream. You are not in the position to tell them whether they are showing it off or how they should spend their money on charity instead. You are also not in the position to judge them. Let them live their life.

Whatever we have in this life is temporary. Feeding your arrogance puts you at risk of losing everything one day, including the good people around you.

❧

Are you the type of person who likes to meddle with others' personal affairs, asking questions like '*When are you getting married?*', '*When will you have a baby?*' or '*It has been ten years, and you still do not have a child?*'

Be self-aware of the words coming out of your mouth. If you have nothing nice to say or ask, then just keep quiet.

Think before you speak. Think once. Think twice. Think three times. And zip it. It is better to be known as someone who is quiet and boring who respects others' privacy than a disrespectful, nosy busybody.

Your caste and position can make you feel that you are in a position of authority and cause you to look down on others. If you are living like this, step back and look at it from the external perspective.

Why are you feeling that way? Is it because you are proud of your status? Is it because you want to feel the sense of belonging to your community? Is it because your community will reject you if you are nice to people? Or is it that you are not confident in yourself if you are not associated with where you belong?

Are those reasons just excuses for you to be impolite to others?

You can react to others' bad behaviour towards you in ways that you deem fit in the moment; however, by default, be respectful of people.

Respect people the way you want others to respect you.

※

Watch your tone of voice when speaking to others and observe their tone of voice when they convey a message to you. Their tone can convey more of a message than their words.

You might notice that your friend has changed physically, such as gaining or losing weight, having a pimple, or any other physical changes. Shut off your opinions and comments. If you are genuinely concerned about their health, instead of commenting directly, you can ask, *'How is life?'* or *'Is everything going well?'*

Be conscious of what you ask others. Do not comment on anything about them that they could not change in a few seconds.

Be open-minded but also be smart to intelligently eliminate unnecessary feedback that you hear.

Karma is not a myth. It is what it is. So, before you do something to someone, stop and think. Karma can happen to you in a matter of seconds.

Be confident when describing yourself to others but also be humble.

Be proud and grateful of your accomplishments and experiences but do not be arrogant.

Be firm when you speak but also speak with respect.

Physical touch is one of the love languages used to express feelings. You can learn to use this appropriately with friends or those you are comfortable with and, more importantly, are comfortable with you.

When I was a teenager, I was really uncomfortable with anyone touching me. I did not like even a friendly hug on my shoulder. A classmate even told me off before, implying that I disliked her, as I swatted her arms away from me.

Over the years, I noticed this but it was never a problem for me. It did not stop me from being friends with anyone. Everyone has their own boundaries.

This all changed after I met a friend 14 years ago, who is now one of my closest friends. Whenever we meet, she will go to the extent of all types of hugging, even while walking, as well as kissing cheeks and forehead, holding hands, intertwining fingers and filling our texts and calls with *I love you* and *I miss you* and *Love* and *Darling*. There might be one or two others who have done this with me over the years, but I don't remember being comfortable enough to similarly respond, like I am with this friend.

Since meeting her, I have totally changed. In fact, whenever I am flirting with people I like, or even when chatting with those I am already comfortable with, I don't feel constrained, and I freely express myself through physical touch.

Surprisingly, this is one way to develop connections with others.

Being charming does not mean you have to be the most gorgeous or handsome person in the eyes of the beholder. A charming personality is as simple as being a good listener, trustworthy, having compassion and having a *'you are yourself'* attitude.

WHEN YOU NEED TO
BE BRAVE
TO LEAVE A RELATIONSHIP

Relationships with people animate our lives.

Having the right partner makes you look forward to waking up each morning.

Being with positive friends makes you look forward to every dinner and outing instead of trying to find an excuse not to go or dragging yourself out to meet them.

This is why it is your responsibility to prioritize who you will allow to be part of your life journey.

ॱᡗ

At times, you may ask yourself if some relationships with your friends, family and co-workers are worth it. If they are not worth your time, why do these people exist in your life in the first place?

You have to reflect on these people and evaluate why they are here with you. Why did you end up with your parents instead of your friends' parents? Is it because their characters fit yours? Is it because you need your kind of parents so that you can achieve your dreams?

With friends, there is more freedom for them to go in and out of your life at any time. They may not always fit into each phase of your life if your character evolves or you have new goals that do not match those of your friends. Then, you have the choice of whether you remain in each other's life.

When you notice a pattern in a person's behaviour, one that you have seen before in someone else, be prepared for the same experience with the new person. The only thing that will help you break the cycle is by changing the outcome.

One time, I felt like a superhero saving my dad from a guy with a similar behavioural pattern as someone we had met before. My parents had forgotten about the previous experience until I reminded them to be careful with the guy.

How did I identify the consistent pattern of behaviour? First, he kept calling my dad about two or three times a week. I don't even call my parents once a week when I am not in town. Second, the conversations leaned towards stories about his mother-in-law, who is my dad's aunt. Third, he tended to highlight all the unpleasant stories of his wife's family that were affecting his marriage. Hmmm … isn't that considered my dad's family? Having the balls to do that was a red flag to me. Fourth, he had a strong desire to be the centre of attention and was grandiose.

One day, after a few months of observing, I had a familiar feeling that something was not right. So, I voiced my opinion to my parents. '*Hey, be careful*', I said. '*Remember that person who was exactly like this? And what happened that time? Wasn't he the one who was lying? And what happened to him now?*' Fortunately, my dad listened to my warning. Gradually, he ignored the guy's phone calls, and a few times, my parents made excuses to prevent him from coming to our place to vent his frustrations. Guess what?

A month later, we found out that this guy divorced his wife and ran away with the money from the sale of his wife's house. That house was bought by his mother-in-law and his wife. Apparently, this was not his first time. After the divorce, he married someone else, divorced again and then married another woman.

This is one peculiar example that made me have faith in my observations and instincts and to be brave enough to act on them regardless of whether the relationship could be affected. Learn to never ignore patterns of behaviour.

When someone tells you they are busy and have no time to text you back, let them be. That is evidence that they are not interested in forging a relationship with you. What do you have to do? Be strong and move on!

There is no correlation between how long you have known someone and the trust you place in them. You can be friends with a person for two decades, but that does not mean you have to be open to telling them everything. Once they have broken your trust, there is no compromise.

People you spend time with shape your personality.

Your friends, co-workers and anyone you spend most of your time with influence the way you think and behave, meaning that your positive and lively behaviour can be influenced by friends who are always filled with negativity and talk about others. If you are not cautious in creating a boundary between you and them, their behaviour will eventually influence you. This is the same scenario when your child mingles with friends who skip school and eventually gets caught one day doing the same with them.

Nothing in your life should be taken for granted, especially your health, wealth and knowledge. The time you are living now is of the essence. Make use of it wisely with the right people.

You can be friendly and say *hello* to anyone, but be particular in who you choose as your close friends and who you spend most of your time with.

Be wary of someone who speaks too much to you about others. Test whether they can be trusted. That is the most important quality in any relationship.

You may have at least one friend who invites you for dinner but throughout the night keeps texting and answering phone calls. The only time she doesn't is when she is sharing stories about herself.

Observe whether this is consistent. If you are concerned, you can ask what is distracting her. If she continues replying to texts from her friends or colleagues, evaluate whether she is interested in hanging out with you.

If someone says they are uncomfortable when they are with you, maybe they cannot handle your energy, which is usually stronger than theirs, either better or worse. Or maybe they don't know how to manage their feelings when they are with you.

These are not problems for you to worry about. Step back if you need to.

Do not bring down your energy of sunshine for people who are mean and self-absorbed.

M

When your group feels awkward during moments of
silence, you are still not comfortable with one another.

Friendship is important only if you and your friends have a mutual understanding about the importance of each other's self-worth.

When your friends start to ignore the importance of respect, not being mindful of what they say to you or not being kind in the way they speak to you, it is time to evaluate the relationship you have with them.

Recently, I had to make this unpleasant decision, which I had seen coming when I started to feel uneasy with a group of friends I had spent time with for about ten years, although usually we only met once a month. The feeling came when one of them kept breaking my trust by saying something to another friend even though I had stated clearly not to say anything until I had told her. It happened about four times in a row within two months.

Another incident was with another friend who purposely said things that I dislike. A phrase that not only I hated, but everyone, including her, hated—*It is time for you to get married since you already know how to cook'*— was embarrassing to me in a social setting.

At our last gathering, I could feel that the energy surrounding me was not good. I told myself to stop justifying everything and this time to *'remember how you were trying to justify reasons for the relationships ten years ago. This is not the same anymore'*.

Be brave when you need to make decisions that will change your friendship with a person. Do not make compromises when others devalue you as a person, whether your friends realize it or not, whether they think it is a joke or not. If you do not consider it to be a joke and most of you feel as if raising the issue will not change anything in your friendship, it is time for you to step back, and sometimes, if you need to, step out.

If you have someone in your life who makes you feel good about yourself, will not say things that hurt your feelings, knows when to joke and when not to (or when they joke, they don't say things that could hurt you), knows their limits, doesn't make you feel timid or bring you down, watches their tone of voice, and genuinely wants to be with you, then you should treasure this person.

Most of the time, when you are in that circle of people, you might not notice the signs of things to come and how these people behave towards you. Or, can I say that is B.S.? You could sense it in the back of your mind, but you are trying to convince yourself to justify your evaluation. Step back. Re-analyse your relationship.

Be friendly but also be selective with who you choose
to spend time with.

Be open to giving yourself opportunities to trust others but also be careful with who you think can be trusted.

Be Brave

WHEN YOU NEED TO
BE BRAVE
TO MOVE ON FROM SOMEONE
YOU ARE IN LOVE WITH

When you love someone, show it because if you don't show your love towards her, how can she know how you feel? Buy her gifts, send food to her home, cook her favourite food or do anything to show your feelings in your own way.

However, when she shows signs of not being interested in you, for whatever reasons, respect her choice. Give her the space and move on.

Love is in abundance. Your love is meant for those who deserve your affection, time and effort.

You can forget a person who has been in your life for years. The question is whether you want to.

Sometimes thinking about that same person gives you comfort. Whatever reasons you have, get back to why you need to forget her and move on. Because if you don't let go, you will not attract new people into your life. When you refuse to let go, you will not meet the person who is really meant for you. You will suffer in silence while she is having a great time with someone else. You will lose that time thinking about her when you can use it to explore new opportunities for yourself.

Come on, you can do it!

ᴎ

Sometimes, a person you have feelings for comes and goes in your life whenever they deem fit for themselves. You have to learn how to evaluate the way you feel about them by asking yourself whether you want them to use you like that forever.

You cannot control them; however, that does not mean you have to be part of their life again when they come back to you.

Moving on from someone can be difficult. It takes all your energy, thinking about them day and night, making you less interested in taking care of yourself, making you shed tears and making you lose your appetite, which can make you lose weight and get that slim figure you have been wanting. But is it worth it? No, it is not worth it!

Get out and find something else that will make you feel excited. Focus on that. Go for that morning walk in the park. Target that 10,000 steps. Go to the gym. Listen to music. Watch movies. Write. You can write poems about her and your relationship and publish the book out of spite. You can compose a song or an entire album about her.

Do something that can release you from that cocoon of overwhelming feelings for her. Remember that there are other more important things you can do in this world than be disappointed and heartbroken forever.

✓

Closure can be in a form of action. There is no need to wait for the right time to talk to them about it.

Closure can be how she responded to one of your texts.

Closure can be when she unfollowed you on Instagram.

Closure can be when she said, '*I will make sure to choose the right friends in the future*'.

Closure need not be telling you that she doesn't feel the same.

Closure need not be a '*let us meet and talk*'.

Relationships are about love and affection, but when there is no respect towards each other's privacy, needs, responsibilities and opinions, then you have to open your eyes, heart and mind. That type of relationship is void of love.

⁊

When a person you are going out with says, '*Ah, I am a nobody since you are more educated and more accomplished than me. I don't think we fit*'. You can reply with, '*Yeah, it's up to you if you want to feel that way. If you have low self-confidence about yourself, then I cannot do anything*'.

There is no need to say anymore if they have a low self-opinion about themselves. It is not your job to make them feel otherwise. This is also the time for you to re-evaluate whether you would like to keep seeing this person because you should not be with someone who has low self-respect towards themselves.

M

In any type of relationship, there is no substitute for respect. It doesn't matter how in love you are, how deep your romance is or how wonderful your intimate moments are. Once your partner raises their hand to you, uses words that are displeasing or demeaning toward you, the love and romance does not mean anything.

Be logical when you are justifying others' actions towards you.

Respect your self-worth.

It can take time to determine a person's character based on their behaviour, and more importantly, whether they are good for you. A nice and exceptional person is not automatically good for you. Your characters might not be a good fit for each other.

When you pray (or even if you are the type who doesn't pray) at the end of the day, say this, '*If this person is not meant for me, can you please let him out of my life? I do not want to waste my time and his time in this relationship*'. This method can be applied to your friends. Your brain and heart have to be in sync when you do this. You need to be open to accepting changes. When you do this, you will be surprised by the results. It could take time for your prayerful request to show results, but most of the time, something will happen immediately.

You can list the qualities of the type of person you want as your partner. Set expectations. Apart from the type of personality you would like in a partner, include the feelings you would like to feel when you are with them. Soon, you will meet that person.

WHEN YOU NEED TO
BE BRAVE
TO CONFIDENTLY RESPOND
TO CERTIFIED IDIOTS

Be careful with the words, voice tonality and volume you use in conversations with people. If you treasure the relationships you have with them, be self-aware of what you say. Think before you say what is in your thoughts.

When her pants are torn, yes, please tell her right away, but do it in private so you will not embarrass her; however, when you notice she has gained weight, looks thinner, or has less stylish hair than normal, learn to control yourself and zip your lips tight. When you are really concerned, you can ask indirect questions, such as *'How have you been?'* or *'Is everything going well?'* If she wants to share her health problems with you, she will; if not, do not be a certified idiot.

Personally, I am the type of person who speaks my mind if I find it necessary in a situation or I want to give a person a piece of my mind. But, most of the time, I am very careful not to hurt my friends' feelings in any way, especially commenting on anything related to physical traits because I have been there. Between the ages of 10 to 12, I gained weight because I loved food. I had no interest in exercising, which is much less fun compared to eating. Friends and relatives made fun of how I looked. That is when I learnt that I do not want to be like them.

There was a friend I used to hang out with in secondary school. She was always made fun of by our schoolmates because of her size. She used to tell me (even though I didn't ask) that she could not shed her weight because she was taking medication at that time. Frankly, I was more concerned about whether she was experiencing any health problems than the size of her body. Because she is still fine to this day, I assume that she is healthy.

After we graduated from secondary school, we met on and off over the years, like every three years. Twenty-three years later, which was our most recent and final meeting, she said to me what those people had said to her without a single consideration to *'stop and think before telling your opinion no one asked for'*.

Most people tell me to ignore unwanted opinions, which is a default response that I normally agree with – but not always. They also suggest being patient. This is also a useful advice. I knew this friend for quite a long time, and apart from this incident, we did have some history outside of this topic. I had already analysed the value of this friendship back to when we were 15, which means that whatever response I gave was justified considering many other factors. How did I respond? I looked at her with firm confidence and smiled with a slight note of sarcasm and with a message in my smile that meant

'*I am not surprised that you are this type of person*'. I replied in my head, '*Of all people, you?*' (I did not say that out loud because it would have crushed her). I said this instead: '*Do you remember what you told me before when your sister said that I always looked slim since I was in school?*' She shook her head. '*This was when I was at your dad's funeral.*' Again, she replied, '*No*'. I said, '*Your response to your sister's compliment towards me was "It is because Sulianah is the boring type". So, when I gained weight, I remembered what you said and reassured myself that it is okay to change. Your body has to change, and it is best to let it be. Every human changes*'. I ended my statement with a slight smirk, while she looked at me stunned in silence.

At that point, I told myself to stop wasting my time committing to a friendship that seemed to be one-sided. I gave her a chance a few years ago, but it seemed to have gone unappreciated.

Be sensitive and evaluate the people you are with. Avoid mingling with friends that could lower your self-esteem. It will break you down. Even though you might have healthy self-esteem, being with people like this will eventually influence the way you think about yourself. You need to be with people who are conscious of their words and use their brains before speaking their minds. Most importantly, when you put in effort to not hurt their feelings, but they do not do the same for you, this is an obvious sign that you should not ignore. Once you start to respect yourself, you will be more sensitive to this kind of treatment.

There will be times, maybe once in every five years or more, when you meet certain people who are older than you. Instead of asking, *'How have you been?'* or *'How is your family?'*, they will comment on how you have changed in an unpleasant way.

First, you can ignore them if they don't mean anything to you. If they do mean something, you will not be seeing them enough for it to matter.

But if you feel like telling them, *'You can do that to others but not to me'*, then you can try this.

Start with a smile. Then, reply with confidence while maintaining your posture, *'Aren't we humans? If we do not change, we are not humans'*. Or, *'Oh, so do you. You look so different now than before. I would like to recommend you this hair dye brand'*. Or, *'Hey I tried this supplement, and it makes a lot of difference to my body. Maybe you should also try it'*.

These possible responses will not make you feel good, but the second one will at least tell the person that you do not appreciate their comments. It will make a difference in how they treat you the next time you meet them. There is a better chance they will speak to you with respect. The best option is that they will avoid talking to you because they are embarrassed or hurt.

There are several factors that could influence someone's behaviour, such as gender, culture, interests, age, motivation, environment, position and situation. They may use these factors as excuses to look down on others.

There are no excuses for raising your voice to a staff member, embarrassing her in front of her colleagues just because you are her manager. Yes, you have the right to reprimand someone for doing something wrong, but with that tone, hmmm … is that your ego speaking? Have you ever stopped to think that your position is not a permanent thing in your life and that in a snap, the tables could turn and you could be treated the same way as you treat your staff? Other than that, are you thinking that by raising your voice, you are trying to prove to them that you are a leader? Instead of getting genuine respect from your team, they are in fact praying that you will be gone soon.

A few years ago, when I was a human resources manager at an engineering company, we employed people from various countries to fill positions, such as engineers, technicians and project managers. There were a few times when I experienced new employees behaving in a peculiarly arrogant way, especially when they talked to me and their new colleagues.

The first thing I did was to not give them any opportunity to cross the line of disrespect.

Then, I shared information about the culture and explained to them how people usually behaves here.

You will be surprised that most people are usually open to learning about the new places they have moved in to and adapting to them.

To know whether someone is a good person, observe how they treat the waitstaff. Simple.

Ten years ago, I ignored this obvious red flag in this group of friends, even though I noticed this when I first started to hang out with them. I knew being disrespectful to the waitstaff or anyone was not right. I don't practice that kind of behaviour. Since I was young, my parents taught me to respect anyone no matter their origin, how they look or their position.

I have the type of character that will not point out someone's bad behaviour, unless they make a scene, which is a different story. They say to act on what you preach. I don't preach, so I act it out. In this case, I exhibited the behaviour that I knew was respectful to show my friends they were wrong. Instead of showing my arrogance, I smiled and spoke nicely to the waitstaff like I always do. Well, it didn't work.

One part of me kept telling myself to get out of the friendship because it was not right. At that time, it was like a sign that something worse might happen. Another part of me was arguing with rational reasons for why my friends treated the waitstaff disrespectfully, telling myself not to be too sensitive and not to be too selective about who I spent my time with. I kid you not, my brain kept overthinking the situation, analysing, evaluating and justifying it again and again. My heart was going in another direction, reminding me not to be too sensitive.

Because I felt guilty, I had several discussions with some friends to justify my analysis: How can a person not have empathy for the servers in restaurants? Is it because that is how they were brought up? Are they too proud of their status? Are they feeding their own ego? Do they act that way to show off their position and wealth? My close friends could not understand, either, because they thought that by default everyone should respect one another.

Over those ten years, the behaviour of this group of friends was consistent and never changed. I made comprises with my justifications. A decade later, one situation (nothing to do with waitstaff) negatively impacted our friendship. The only quote I could recite to myself was, '*I told you so*'.

There are differences between criticism, feedback and comments that you never asked for. Be sensitive in differentiating between these so that you can evaluate who you should hold on to in your life. When someone says that you are too sensitive to accept criticism, don't merely agree with that person.

First, you are in the position to evaluate whether you asked for the comments in the first place.

Second, a person with pure intentions will not start with a negative sentence. They will not use a tone of voice that could strike a nerve. I have a handful of friends who use words intelligently. They know people are observant and sensitive when a tone is not sincere or when it is filled with sarcasm. They will start a conversation in a way that will make me want to speak based on what I am comfortable sharing.

Third, if you do not feel like responding to them because you are respecting their position or relationship status but still do not want to listen to them, step back and excuse yourself from that person or group. Prioritize yourself and put your own feelings first. There is no need to think about whether it is rude or hurtful to them. If you want to stay, it is up to you. But, like I said in my introduction, I am not censoring the practicality of my motivational quotes.

Fourth, reply to them in a composed and firm way. You can directly reply to them or ask intelligent questions in return. For instance, if the person said, '*You are too sensitive. You should listen when someone says you are stubborn so that you can improve*'. Possible ways to reply would be, '*Oh, you think I am stubborn? Can you give me an example so I can look into it?*' I'll bet you most of the time, they cannot come up with a concrete example. Another way to reply could be, '*Yes, yes, you might be right. I will look into that. Since you are concerned about me, I would like to suggest one thing about you that you can improve on*'. With this sentence, you know that you have struck a nerve.

There is a quote that says, '*The only way to make a man trustworthy is to trust him*'. This is true; however, whenever you feel like your lips are sealed when you intend to tell someone your opinion, follow that lead. Zip it up. You will not regret it.

Why?

Because when you feel like saying something to that person, but your lips are sealed, an incident will prove that you made the right decision to keep your thoughts to yourself.

Learn to differentiate between someone who is keen to learn from you or who wants to use the information to discredit your beliefs.

When he is using the opportunity to humiliate your hope, it is better to avoid discussion because he has no intention of listening.

Defend yourself when you need to, but if you observe that a person is testing your patience, step back and don't waste your time. He is not interested in your point of view.

When you are telling someone something and they interrupt you, take a deep breath and stop talking. Don't share something of importance to you with someone who is not interested. You know that whatever you need to say is highly valuable to you. Do not degrade its importance for someone else who is not interested.

There are times that you need to tell a person, '*Enough is enough*'. For instance, when someone keeps telling you to settle down and this pisses you off, handle this intelligently. You can entertain them with respect by keeping quiet, ignoring them and moving on.

Another way that might help to shut them up so they will not say this over and over whenever you meet is to question them with logical scenarios. Ask them, '*Will you pay for my wedding expenses?*', '*Will you bear the responsibilities if we divorce?*' or '*Will you pay for my children's school fees?*'

They will usually end up laughing, the laughter of embarrassment.

If someone tells you to wear something you are uncomfortable in, for instance if you are not the type of person who wears dresses, it is your choice to not follow their demands.

You can tell them, '*Since you want me to wear something that I am not comfortable in, why don't you wear those shorts?*' or '*I don't like the way you keep repeating this to me. I would appreciate it if you stopped telling me to wear something I am not comfortable in*'.

I had a friend who always told me to wear clothes that were not my style. At first, it sounded like a joke, so I ignored it. When it happened many times over a ten-year period, I was really pissed off. Every time it happened, I kept reminding myself loud and clear, '*Why are you still justifying this, and why are you ignoring it?*'

If someone you know feels embarrassed to walk beside you just because of the way you look, you have the choice to make yourself look better or not. It is up to you.

Choose to change because you think and feel like it. After you are comfortable with the changes to your appearance, don't mingle with them like you used to. They don't deserve you.

You may notice on many occasions that your boss does not pay attention when you are talking to him, especially about important matters that need his full attention. He may be busy with his laptop and not even look at you. It is frustrating and you feel that he is not acknowledging your presence.

How can you handle this?

One way is to stop talking immediately. The absence of your voice will make him look up from his laptop, wondering why you suddenly stopped talking. Or, you can say to him, *'It seems like you are busy. I will come back later'*.

Be firm when you speak. Stand up and get ready to leave. Share your thoughts and ideas only when you have his full attention.

Lending money or anything of value to others can be a frustrating experience. I have personal experiences and have heard stories of how other people were also trapped in this dilemma. People often think, '*I too need this money, but if I don't lend it to my friend, will it affect our friendship?*'

Are the following phrases familiar to you: '*I promise I will pay you back next week*', '*I will transfer the money to you now*' and '*I will get my salary at the end of this month, and I will pay you back immediately?*' When someone convinces you that they can be trusted and they will return the money to you on time, rest assured that there is no guarantee that you will get it back.

A few years ago, a friend who was a senior at my high school contacted me by chance after he saw a photo of me with one of my close friends from university, whom he apparently knew back then. One day, he texted me, saying his mum was in the hospital, and he needed money to pay for her hospitalization fees. I asked him many questions, even though I already knew he was not being honest with me. The way he portrayed himself at the time was the same pattern as someone I met years ago. That person was the last person I lent money to, and I learnt the lesson to be cautious about trusting anyone. So, this friend kept negotiating with me, even though I had already given him the excuse that I need to pay for my school fees and daily expenses. I said, '*I don't have money. I cannot help you*'. Take note, people who want to borrow money from you do not care about your needs. Everything is all about them.

Instead of the $750 that he was asking for, I said I could only give him $50. You may ask, '*Well, why did you cave in if you already knew you may not get it back?*' Remember that close friend of mine? There was some reasoning in my mind about her being our mutual friend, and I was justifying not wanting my selfishness to affect our friendship. I did not even care about my friendship with the guy asking for the money. Yes, that reasoning had no connection, but my emotions were directing my mind to believe that my decision would affect my relationship with my close friend.

Eventually, I gave him $50, but in the back of my mind, I was prepared that if he did not return the money, I would not regret my decision. As most storylines of lending and borrowing go, a one-month deadline was extended by days, weeks and months. The usual popular one-liners used by these shameless certified idiots are: '*I promise next week*' or '*I promise tomorrow*'.

A few months later, my close friend texted me and said,

'I would like to ask you something. I want to know whether he has borrowed money from you because he borrowed $750 from me and keeps giving a lot of excuses about paying it back'.

Surprise! To cut this story short, we decided to go to his house. He was not home, but his mum was. She was healthy, not hospitalized and never was hospitalized. Clearly, she was his bait. We were lucky during that time that his mum and sister helped us settle the case then and there after we had explained both of our stories.

So, what are some lessons about dealing with shameless people who want to borrow money from you? Don't think. Stop yourself from reading texts they send about their story, and don't bother analysing it. Immediately reply, wait a day or two or even ignore it all together. Reply with a *'No, I don't have it'*. Be firm. There is no need to apologize or give them any reasons about why you cannot help. If you would like to ignore their text, why not? There are no rules saying you need to reply.

When someone asks to borrow money because they need to buy groceries for their family to feed their children, don't think too much. Your reply can be, *'I don't have money to help, but I can buy some groceries and arrange to send them to your home'*. Most of the time, they will reply, *'It is okay. I prefer money'*. Why? Because the money they asked for is not for their groceries. I suggested this method to a friend, and that person replied to my friend with these exact words: *'It is okay.*

I prefer money instead.

There are various reasons you may be inclined to cave in. You might want attention from or to be accepted by this person who wants to borrow money from you. If they look decent, nice, handsome, pretty or charming, these qualities may distract you from looking at the situation from a logical perspective.

Why do you need attention from someone like this? Why do you need to feel accepted by this person? Do you think he or she cares about you? Stop evaluating.

Those who ask for your money usually do not need it because they are poor or starving. If you don't believe me, go check their social media photos and status updates. They are travelling, aren't they? She bought a guitar for her son, didn't she? She wears expensive perfume, doesn't she? He just renovated his home, didn't he?

If you are a woman and a man asks to borrow money from you, he is not *The One* or not your friend. If your friend would like to borrow money from you, she is not your real friend who can be trusted. The one who really needs help will do their best to not bother you. Yes, I stand by what I say here.

Lending money to people 'in need' is supposedly a kind deed, but most of the time, it destroys relationships and the one who feels like a borrower is you instead. The actions of one person may cause you to develop distrust towards others who may not deserve it.

If you want to be kind or rack up good deeds, use your

money wisely for those who need it the most. Donate to charity. Visit houses of people in need and donate food to them. Buy food for homeless people. Give shelter to people in need. Donate food to an orphanage. Sponsor education. Buy books for children in need. Send groceries to an old folks' home.

Value your hard-earned money. Don't be concerned if someone says you are stingy. All that matters is that you know who you are.

Be smart and learn to be selective.

The word 'no' exists in the dictionary. You are allowed to use it for any circumstances that you deem fit, especially with people who are selfish, are not trustworthy or whom you do not intend to communicate with.

There are differences between being disrespectful and insensitive and comedic. Using your character weaknesses or those of others and the stories and experiences shared in a group to joke and be sarcastic is clearly not funny. There are professional terms for this—opportunistic, cunning, deceitful and rude.

When someone adds the one-liners '*Trust me*' or '*Believe me*' to most of their sentences, don't!

I used to work with someone who was one example of a handful of people I have met who used these phrases every time they needed anyone to believe them. When he reported on what happened at the worksite, he used these words most of the time in his conversation for updates on how everyone was doing and how the project was going. Well, 99.9% of the time, his updates were the opposite of what really happened at the site. Do not be blindsided by these phrases.

When a person raises their voice at you for no reason, even if you make a mistake, you must learn to respond. There is a certain tone of voice that is indicative that they are looking down on you. For instance, if your superior speaks to you in a tone of voice that is demeaning to your position, such as *'You should have called them, right?'*, *'Isn't that your job?'*, *'What have you been doing all day?'* or *'Can't you solve this kind of problem?'*, be brave enough to reply in a tone of voice that will make them stop behaving like that towards you. Be bold and do not feel timid or inferior. Maintain a steady voice.

Make eye contact. Be confident. Do not look down or divert your eyes away from them. Do not smile. Breathe. Maintain your voice. Then, reply with whatever you have in mind, like *'What makes you think I was not working all day?'*, *'This is the work that I completed'* or *'Yes, I did call them, and there was no reply. So, I sent an email. Come look at this'*. Be firm. Have the evidence in your hand to make sure they do not have the opportunity to pinpoint anything else. This method works.

At times, you will be put in a spot by someone to do things they think are right from their perspective. They will use phrases like *'You should do this'*, *'You shouldn't do this'*, *'Why are you stubborn? You should do it this way'*, *'You should be like that person'* or *'If I were you, I would reply like this'*.

Again, by default, you can keep it to yourself and ignore them, but why keep it to yourself and worry that it will be hurtful to them when they don't care about how you feel? Question them in the same way by saying things like *'You should do this'*, *'You shouldn't do this'*, *'Why are you stubborn? You should do it this way'*, *'You should be like that person'*, *'Why should I listen to you when you never listen to my advice?'*, *'Didn't I say the same thing?'*, *'If you were in that situation, you would do it worse than I did'* or *'You will not have the balls to even say anything to him like I did'*.

Years ago, a younger cousin of mine asked my opinion about furthering her studies because I had just started the first year of my bachelor's degree. Other than my dad, I was the first third generation in my family to have achieved that level of education. While having a discussion with her, an uncle of ours interrupted our conversation, saying, '*Well, a woman will end up in the kitchen anyway when they are married.*'

At that time, I was less confident in my ability to argue and to challenge someone older, so I kept my opinions to myself and ignored him. I was sizzling inside! I vented my disbelief by complaining to my parents about how someone could be so narrow-minded, selfish and backwards-thinking. He should encourage his nieces or keep his mouth shut.

I ignored his opinions and still do my thing with an additional vision in place. I told myself that I will make sure I will be featured in the national newspaper when I graduate to make my uncle mad and to debunk his negative opinions.

Three years later, on my graduation day, I was called by the university's marketing department to ask if they could feature my graduation story in the newspaper. And it happened.

If anyone has the balls to say these things to me now, my replies will be, '*Then, why are you sending your daughter to school? Waste of money, right?*' or '*Maybe it is time for you to stop sending your grandchildren to kindergarten. They don't need it*'.

Stay focused. Shut out unnecessary 'white noise'. When you have a dream to follow and goals to achieve in your life, learn to ignore others so you can do your own thing. Don't allow others' points of view to create a bottleneck to your goals. It is your responsibility to filter anything that comes into your life and to have a quality experience for yourself.

My aim to *Be Brave* and to do the things I want is the result of the vision I have for myself. Sharing these quotes and stories in this book is one of my dreams accomplished, and you reading every single word I wrote is a satisfying experience and truly an honour for me.

Similarly, I hope that you achieve everything you wish for, even those dreams beyond your wildest imagination. Your thoughts and feelings are boundless, so be open to new experiences and to meeting new people.

ABOUT THE AUTHOR

S. Sulianah is an author of poetry and personality growth books and articles. She is also the founder of Grapholistic International. Over the last twenty years, S.Sulianah has been practicing graphology and educating people about the science behind it and how it influences human personality development. By engaging in fieldwork in human resource management with organisations for nearly 20 years, she has been using the science of graphology for recruitment and personnel management.

She is also a trained and certified personality growth coach, mainly focusing on the area of personality development for building positive self-esteem and self-confidence. Her coaching sessions incorporate the use of graphotherapy (changing handwriting to improve a trait) to maximize the benefits of her sessions for her clients. S.Sulianah is known for her engaging energy when presenting informative topics to audiences and she is able to tailor her presentations to clients' needs.

S.Sulianah's postgraduate training and continuing education has been in human behaviour, marketing, consumer insights, business management, mindset and handwriting analysis. She has a Bachelor of Arts degree specializing in Psychology & Marketing Management from Murdoch University, Australia. She has undergone

certification in Disruptive Strategy with Clayton Christensen at HBX Harvard Business School. She has attended lectures on personnel and children's handwriting at the London College of Graphology and has a diploma in handwriting analysis from ICS. She also received a Master of Science degree in Marketing and Consumer Insights at Nanyang Technological University in Singapore. The premise of her research is based on her beliefs that high self-esteem is a catalyst for positive emotions and eliminating self-doubts.

When not writing, she spends her time reading, travelling, producing her podcasts, analysing handwriting and coaching.

Uncensored Motivational Quotes

9 789811 821851